BLACK LIVES MATTER:
Grassroots Movement
to Global Phenomenon

About the Author

Stuart A. Kallen is the author of more than 350 nonfiction books for children and young adults. He has written on topics ranging from the theory of relativity to the art of electronic dance music. In 2018 Kallen won a Green Earth Book Award from the Nature Generation environmental organization for his book *Trashing the Planet: Examining the Global Garbage Glut*. In his spare time, he is a singer, songwriter, and guitarist in San Diego.

© 2021 ReferencePoint Press, Inc.
Printed in the United States

For more information, contact:
ReferencePoint Press, Inc.
PO Box 27779
San Diego, CA 92198
www.ReferencePointPress.com

Picture Credits:
Cover: ChameleonsEye/Shutterstock.com
 5: Associated Press
10: Associated Press
13: mimagephotography/Shutterstock.com
17: Crush Rush/Shutterstock.com
25: BradleyStearn/Shutterstock.com
30: Christos S/Shutterstock.com
34: Massimo Giachetti/iStock
41: Associated Press
45: DisobeyArt/Shutterstock.com
48: Bridgeman Picture Archive
51: Bryan Regan/Shutterstock.com

LIBRARY OF CONGRESS CATALOGING-IN-PUBLICATION DATA

Names: Kallen, Stuart A., 1955- author.
Title: Black lives matter : grassroots movement to global phenomenon / by
  Stuart A. Kallen.
Description: San Diego, CA : ReferencePoint Press, 2021. | Series: Being
  Black in America | Includes bibliographical references and index.
Identifiers: LCCN 2020043181 (print) | LCCN 2020043182 (ebook) | ISBN
  9781678200244 (library binding) | ISBN 9781678200251 (ebook)
Subjects: LCSH: Black lives matter movement--Influence--Juvenile
  literature. | African Americans--Civil rights--History--21st
  century--Juvenile literature. | United States--Race relations--Juvenile
  literature. | Racial profiling in law enforcement--United
  States--Juvenile literature. | African Americans--Social
  conditions--21st century--Juvenile literature. | Racism--United
  States--Juvenile literature.
Classification: LCC E185.86 .K27 2021 (print) | LCC E185.86 (ebook) | DDC
  323.1196/073--dc23
LC record available at https://lccn.loc.gov/2020043181
LC ebook record available at https://lccn.loc.gov/2020043182

CONTENTS

Good Trouble

In June 2020 the Washington, DC, street that leads directly to the White House got a makeover: Sixteenth Street NW was renamed Black Lives Matter Plaza. To commemorate the event, the street was painted with 35-foot-tall (10.7 m) yellow letters that read "Black Lives Matter." Two days later congressional representative and civil rights icon John Lewis visited Black Lives Matter Plaza. It was an emotional moment: the eighty-year-old representative had been fighting for racial equality in the United States for more than six decades. Lewis was dying of cancer, and his visit to Black Lives Matter Plaza was his last public appearance. He died the following month.

Lewis has exerted a powerful influence on young activists since he began organizing demonstrations in 1960 at age twenty. During the civil rights era, Lewis was beaten, brutalized, and arrested on several occasions for starting what he called "good trouble." This type of trouble, according to Lewis, leads to greater equality for Black people. Patrisse Cullors, one of the founders of Black Lives Matter (BLM), is among the many people inspired by Lewis's call to fight for racial justice. Cullors says:

> He was a young, radical Black man who was challenging not just the status quo in government, but also the older leadership in the movement. And I felt really moved by him. . . . [Lewis was] brutalized fighting for a more equitable America, for Black people in particular. And so, we

fast forward to 2020, when we have been in the streets, and the same tactics of the police being used against us as a way to deter us from fighting for Black freedom. And yet, that never deterred Congressman Lewis.[1]

Future generations might see the founders of Black Lives Matter in much the same way that Lewis is revered today. Millions of people throughout the world rallied under the BLM banner in 2020 to protest the injustice of police killings of Black Americans. They lay down in the street for Breonna Taylor, who was shot to death in a botched police raid in Louisville, Kentucky. Protesters took a knee for Elijah McClain, choked to death by police in Aurora, Colorado. And BLM supporters endured tear gas and rubber bullets for George Floyd, who died after a Minneapolis officer knelt on his neck for nearly nine minutes.

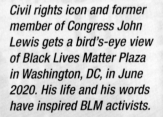

Civil rights icon and former member of Congress John Lewis gets a bird's-eye view of Black Lives Matter Plaza in Washington, DC, in June 2020. His life and his words have inspired BLM activists.

A New Power Network

Black Lives Matter was founded by activists Cullors, Alicia Garza, and Opal Tometi in 2013 as a hashtag meant to draw attention to police brutality and racially motivated violence perpetrated against Black people. The group rose to prominence the following year when authorities in Ferguson, Missouri, shot a young Black man, Michael Brown, as he walked down the street. Since that time Black Lives Matter has blossomed into a worldwide phenomenon that has been the driving force behind thousands of nonviolent protests against systemic racism in the United States and else-where. Protesters sympathetic to the BLM cause marched in hundreds of cities in Europe, the Middle East, Asia, Africa, and South and Central America. They demanded justice for Black people in the United States while calling for an end to police brutality and systemic racism in their own countries.

During these protests—which continue today—a new generation of grassroots activists has turned to social media for organizing and advocacy. And in many cases teenage organizers have spearheaded protests. Singer Alicia Keys credits the deft use of social media for BLM's success: "Imagine if Martin Luther King and Malcolm X had Instagram. It would have been a whole other power network."[2]

> "Imagine if Martin Luther King and Malcolm X had Instagram. It would have been a whole other power network."[2]
>
> —Alicia Keys, singer

This new power network seems to have galvanized and increased public support in ways not seen in decades. In a 2016 Pew poll of US voters, 43 percent of Americans said they supported or strongly supported the Black Lives Matter movement. Four years later, after the start of protests over Floyd's killing by police, Pew reported that 67 percent of all Americans supported or strongly supported the movement.

Black Americans have long understood the look and feel of systemic racism. The same 2020 Pew poll revealed that 83 percent of Black Americans have experienced discrimination based on their race. They have been stopped by police for no reason, treated unfairly when seeking medical treatment, and singled out for their race when shopping. Almost all have had racist slurs hurled at them. Yet the time for real change might have finally arrived. Just days before he died, Lewis wrote a short essay encouraging young Black Lives Matter activists to confront racism and racial violence with love and peaceful protest: "When historians pick up their pens to write the story of the 21st century, let them say that it was your generation who laid down the heavy burdens of hate at last and that peace finally triumphed."[3]

CHAPTER ONE

#BlackLivesMatter

In 2014 it seemed as if Americans had finally awakened to the racism that has long been a part of daily life for Black people. And the awakening occurred in a place that few people had ever heard of, Ferguson, Missouri. This majority-Black city located near St. Louis had a population of around twenty-one thousand. On August 9, 2014, a White police officer, Darren Wilson, fatally shot an unarmed eighteen-year-old Black man named Michael Brown. The events that unfolded after the shooting exposed an uncomfortable truth that had been widely known to Black Americans but less so to many White Americans: police in the United States often discriminate against people of color.

The encounter that led to Brown's death began when he and a friend were walking in the street. Wilson drove by and ordered them to move onto the sidewalk. Brown refused. This led to a brief altercation at the police car that resulted in Brown getting shot in the hand. Brown took off running as Wilson ran after him, firing more shots. Brown turned around with his hands raised and told Wilson that he was unarmed. At this time Wilson fired his weapon at least six times, striking Brown and killing him. The officer later said that he fired in self-defense because Brown was charging at him, ready to attack.

After the shooting, Brown's body lay in the street for more than four hours. Cell phone images of this scene went viral on Twitter. The next night crowds gathered for a candlelight vigil in the spot where Brown had died. Organizers called for peaceful protest, but some participants vandalized vehicles and looted local businesses. Around 150 police officers arrived, dressed in full riot gear. Dozens of protesters were arrested, but the protests continued for more than a week. Authorities responded with military-style tactics. Rifle-carrying police in body armor patrolled in armored personnel carriers. They fired tear gas at demonstrators and blasted acoustic weapons meant to cause ear-splitting pain. Police also shot protesters with rubber bullets, which can cause injuries ranging from mild bruising to serious bone fractures and, in some cases, death.

The Ferguson unrest attracted widespread attention. On social media, hashtags including #HandsUpDontShoot and #NoJusticeNoPeace drove even more protesters into the streets. Another hashtag that dominated social media and was seen on dozens of signs held by protesters was #BlackLivesMatter. Few people had seen or heard that expression at the time, but in a matter of weeks the phrase "Black lives matter" provided a unifying message wherever social justice protests were held.

The Disease of Racism

The phrase "Black lives matter" first emerged on social media in 2013, after a jury rendered a not guilty verdict in the shooting death of a Black teenager. The shooting occurred on the night of February 26, 2012. Seventeen-year-old Trayvon Martin was walking home after visiting a convenience store in Sanford, Florida. Martin was confronted by a neighborhood watch coordinator named George Zimmerman. Zimmerman later told police that he thought Martin, who was wearing a black hoodie, looked suspicious. After a momentary scuffle, Zimmerman shot and killed Martin. Zimmerman was arrested after the shooting but was quickly released. Although Martin was unarmed, Zimmerman told police he acted in self-defense.

Thousands of people attended rallies to protest Martin's death. Zimmerman was eventually charged with murder, but during a closely watched trial in July 2013, he was acquitted of the charge. President Barack Obama weighed in on the verdict: "When Trayvon Martin was first shot, I said that this could have been my son. Another way of saying that is Trayvon Martin could have been me 35 years ago. . . . I think it's important to recognize that the African American community is looking at this issue through a set of experiences and a history that doesn't go away."[4]

When California community activist Alicia Garza learned of Zimmerman's acquittal, she said she felt like she had been punched in the gut. She woke up thinking about it and crying in the middle of the night. Garza channeled her pain into what she

A protester confronts Missouri State Highway Patrol troopers who have been stationed in front of the Ferguson police station during August 2014 protests over the police shooting of Michael Brown.

called a love note to Black people: "Black people. I love you. I love us. Our lives matter. Black Lives Matter."[5] Garza posted her love letter on Facebook, and it attracted immediate attention. In Southern California one of Garza's close friends, Patrisse Cullors, shared the message with the hashtag #BlackLivesMatter. In New York City another friend, immigration rights organizer Opal Tometi, was inspired to contact Garza after she saw the post: "There [was] a lot of rage, a lot of pain, a lot of cynicism. But her post resonated with me, for a number of reasons. I think it being explicitly black, it being a message rooted in love, and it just felt very hopeful."[6] Tometi called Garza and offered to create a social media platform called Black Lives Matter, which would utilize the slogan to launch a new civil rights movement.

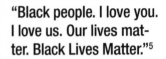

"Black people. I love you. I love us. Our lives matter. Black Lives Matter."[5]

—Alicia Garza, cofounder of Black Lives Matter

Valuing Some Lives over Others

The names Trayvon Martin and Michael Brown will forever be linked through the Black Lives Matter movement. Although the two young men never met, they shared some things in common during their tragically short lives—experiences that are common to millions of other Black Americans in every part of the United States. Brown and Martin lived in a country where glaring racial inequality was built into nearly every aspect of their existence. According to figures compiled by the public policy organization Brookings Institution, the average White family in 2020 held ten times more wealth than the average Black family. Blacks were twice as likely as Whites to lack health insurance and three times more likely to live in poverty. And Black people continue to be treated with suspicion by authorities whether they are shopping, going to school, driving, or simply walking down the street.

These problems are commonly referred to as systemic racism. This term defines racial discrimination that is deeply embedded in the agencies and organizations that oversee criminal justice, education, health care, politics, employment, and other aspects of society. African American studies professor Eddie S. Glaude Jr. describes systemic racism as a value gap, the idea that White people are valued more than Blacks:

> We talk about the achievement gap in education or the wealth gap between white Americans and other groups, but the value gap reflects something more basic: that no matter our stated principles or how much progress we think we've made, white people are valued more than others in this country, and that fact continues to shape the life chances of millions of [Black] Americans.[7]

Laws to Harass Black People

African Americans have plenty of experience with racial bias in the criminal justice system, beginning with interactions with police. A 2019 study of 100 million police traffic stops by Stanford University shows that Black drivers across the United States were twice as likely to be pulled over by police compared to White drivers. Blacks were four times more likely to be searched for drugs or weapons. The authors of the study concluded that these figures revealed evidence of widespread discrimination in police decisions to stop and search drivers. Many Black Americans have a derisive term for this discrimination. They say there were pulled over for DWB, or driving while Black.

"No matter our stated principles or how much progress we think we've made, white people are valued more than others in this country."[7]

—Eddie S. Glaude Jr., African American studies professor

In 2015 the *New York Times* examined tens of thousands of traffic stops in North Carolina, one of six states that collected this type of data at that time. The newspaper's investigation included personal stories from African Americans who described being

Studies show that Black drivers are twice as likely as White drivers to be pulled over by police and four times as likely to be searched for drugs or weapons. Black Americans sometimes refer to this as DWB, or driving while Black.

harassed by police in the city of Greensboro. The investigation shone a harsh light on the problems facing drivers who say their only offense was driving while Black. According to reporters Sharon LaFraniere and Andrew W. Lehren, "Officers were more likely to stop black drivers for no discernable reason. And they were more likely to use force if the driver was black, even when they did not encounter physical resistance."[8]

The report described cases of Black motorists who were wrongly accused of reckless driving, drunk driving, drug possession, and prostitution during routine traffic stops. Cars were searched, and people were arrested and jailed on false charges. Those who objected to aggressive police behavior were pepper sprayed, Tasered, or beaten. Greensboro civil rights attorney Lewis Pitts was not surprised by these findings: "[If a Black motorist] does anything but be completely submissive and cower, then you get the classic countercharge by the officer that there was resistance, or disorderly conduct, or public intoxication. Then they end up in jail."[9]

Militarized Police

After New York City and Washington, DC, were attacked by terrorists on September 11, 2001, the mission for police departments across the country rapidly expanded. In addition to policing their local communities, authorities were expected to respond to terrorist threats. As a result, police departments were militarized. The US government supplied around eight thousand local departments with more than $5 billion worth of military-grade equipment, including machine guns, grenade launchers, night-vision sniper rifles, and even military helicopters and armored tanks and personnel carriers.

Many Americans were made aware of this policy for the first time during the 2014 Black Lives Matter protests in Ferguson. Images on the nightly news and social media sites showed tanks rolling through the streets bristling with police in full riot gear, armed with weapons of war. The response generated widespread criticism since police are not usually trained to use military weapons. As Attorney General Eric Holder wrote in 2014, "At a time when we must seek to rebuild trust between law enforcement and the local community, I am deeply concerned that the deployment of military equipment and vehicles sends a conflicting message. The law enforcement response to these demonstrations must seek to reduce tensions, not heighten them."

Quoted in Marisol Bello and Yamiche Alcindor, "Police in Ferguson Ignite Debate About Military Tactics," *USA Today*, August 14, 2014. www.usatoday.com.

While the *New York Times* focused on one state, the situation in Greensboro was not unique. A 2014 study of thirty-five hundred police departments by *USA Today* found that 95 percent of them arrested Black people at a higher rate than other groups. And police encounters can have deadly consequences for Black people. While the circumstances behind each stop are unique, an average of thirty Black people are shot by police during traffic stops each year. This makes traffic stops the most dangerous interactions Black people can have with police.

It is not just traffic stops that pose a danger to African Americans. According to an investigation by the *Washington Post*, police nationwide have fatally shot about one thousand people each year since 2015, when the newspaper began gathering this data. When those deaths are broken down by race, the newspaper concludes, the statistics show that "the rate at which black Americans are killed by police is more than twice as high as the rate for white Americans."[10] Black males were three times more likely to be killed by police than White males. And one in every thousand Black men can expect to be killed by police. In another study, the *Washington Post* found that no officers were convicted, even when people were shot under questionable circumstances. These statistics are a cause for despair, as journalist Julia Craven writes: "Like a number of black people, I am traumatized by this—to the point where I expect there to be no justice, no ramifications, no [cares] given when a black person is killed by a police officer. Every time this happens, my stomach twists into knots. I want to scream."[11]

> "Like a number of black people, I am traumatized by [police killings]—to the point where I expect there to be no justice, no ramifications, no [cares] given when a black person is killed by a police officer."[11]
>
> —Julia Craven, journalist

A Livestream Killing

Statistics like these paint a broad and disturbing picture. But it was yet another shooting that brought Black Lives Matter activists and their supporters back onto the streets. In July 2016, in the St. Paul, Minnesota, suburb of Falcon Heights, police pulled over a thirty-two-year-old Black man named Philando Castile. He was accompanied by his girlfriend, Diamond Reynolds, and her four-year-old daughter. Castile's car had a broken taillight, which attracted the attention of police officer Jeronimo Yanez. After the stop, Castile told Yanez he was in possession of a firearm, which he was licensed to carry. When Castile reached into his pocket for his driver's license, Yanez fired seven shots into the car. Five of the bullets hit Castile, killing him.

Like many police shootings, this one might have gone largely unnoticed by the public. But Reynolds livestreamed the aftermath of the encounter on Facebook. The graphic video shows Castile slumped in the car, dying from chest wounds. Reynolds later explained why she livestreamed the event: "I did it so that the world knows that these police are not here to protect and serve us. They are here to assassinate us. They are here to kill us because we are black."[12]

The Facebook post triggered large local protests within hours. The next day Minnesota governor Mark Dayton released a statement: "Would this have happened if those passengers, the driver and the passengers, were white? I don't think it would have. . . . I think all of us in Minnesota are forced to confront that this kind of racism exists."[13] By this time activists working with Black Lives Matter and other groups had organized demonstrations throughout the country to protest Castile's shooting. In Oakland, California, over one thousand demonstrators shut down Interstate 880 for several hours. In Minneapolis demonstrators blocked Interstate 94.

In Dallas a peaceful protest turned deadly when Black military veteran Micah Xavier Johnson ambushed a group of police officers. Police, who later studied Johnson's social media posts, claimed he was angry about recent police shootings and wanted to kill White people. Johnson shot and killed five Dallas police officers and wounded nine others before he was killed.

Johnson was described as a loner who was sympathetic to the BLM cause. But Johnson had no known connection to Black Lives Matter, which drew thousands of peaceful protesters to Dallas that day. And while many BLM supporters offered condolences to the families of the murdered officers and expressed shock and sadness over the shootings, there were worries that the actions of one person might overshadow the movement's message. A post on the Black Lives Matter website attempted to address this issue: "[The shooting of Dallas police officers] is a tragedy—both for those who have been impacted by yesterday's attack and for our democracy. . . . There are some who would use these

Thousands take part in a March for Our Lives protest in 2018 in Columbia, South Carolina. This student-led movement has taken inspiration from Black Lives Matter, says BLM cofounder Patrisse Cullors.

events to stifle a movement for change and quicken the demise of a vibrant discourse on the human rights of Black Americans. We should reject all of this."[14]

Despite this setback, Black Lives Matter stayed focused on its goal: calling attention to ongoing racial injustice and bringing about change. Protests were held in many cities. By July 2016 there were 112 demonstrations in 88 American cities. Black Lives Matter received high-profile attention when four National Basketball Association superstars expressed their support for the movement at the televised ESPY Awards show, which celebrates excellence in sports. LeBron James, Dwyane Wade, Carmelo Anthony, and Chris Paul each issued a call to action from the awards stage. They asked athletes to renounce violence and join the movement to stop racial injustice. Wade said, "The racial profiling has to stop. The shoot-to-kill mentality has to stop. Not seeing the value in black and brown bodies has to stop."[15] Wade also called for an end to gang violence in places like Chicago and Dallas.

Sparking Resistance

Black Lives Matter celebrated its fifth anniversary in 2018. By that time the BLM hashtag had been used 30 million times on Twitter. In an interview marking the anniversary, Cullors described BLM's impact on other social causes—among them the March for Our Lives antigun movement founded after the 2018 shootings that killed seventeen students and staff at Marjory Stoneman Douglas

President Obama on Trayvon Martin

In July 2013 President Barack Obama weighed in on the shooting of Trayvon Martin in Sanford, Florida, by neighborhood watch volunteer George Zimmerman. Obama described the casual racism he and other Black Americans commonly experience in their daily lives:

> There are very few African American men in this country who haven't had the experience of being followed when they were shopping in a department store. That includes me. There are very few African American men who haven't had the experience of walking across the street and hearing the locks click on the doors of cars. That happens to me—at least before I was a senator. There are very few African Americans who haven't had the experience of getting on an elevator and a woman clutching her purse nervously and holding her breath until she had a chance to get off. That happens often. . . .

> Those sets of experiences inform how the African American community interprets what happened [to Trayvon Martin] in Florida. And it's inescapable for people to bring those experiences to bear. The African American community is also knowledgeable that there is a history of racial disparities in the application of our criminal laws— everything from the death penalty to enforcement of our drug laws.

Barack Obama, "Remarks by the President on Trayvon Martin," White House, July 19, 2013. https://obama whitehouse.archives.gov.

High School in Parkland, Florida. She said, "[BLM] has popularized civil disobedience and the need to put our bodies on the line. . . . With things like the Women's March, and Me Too, and March for our Lives, all of these movements, their foundations are in Black Lives Matter."[16]

Black Lives Matter remained controversial after its first five years. Those who did not support the movement pointed out that police have an extremely difficult job. Officers have to deal with many of the failures of modern American society, including homelessness, drug addiction, gang violence, domestic violence, terrorism, and a nation awash in guns. While these kinds of issues seem unsolvable, many believe that the value gap that prompted the establishment of Black Lives Matter can be closed. And the activists and supporters of Black Lives Matter are not planning to rest until systemic racism in the criminal justice system is addressed at the highest levels of government and at the street level, where daily interactions with police can turn a simple traffic stop into a deadly encounter.

CHAPTER TWO

A Force to Be Reckoned With

It was the cry heard around the world. George Floyd begging for his life as Minneapolis police officer Derek Chauvin knelt on his neck: "I can't breathe."[17] Floyd—handcuffed and facedown in the street—repeated these three words over and over as three other police officers stood and watched. Multiple people who were there captured those moments in cell phone videos even as they begged Chauvin to get up. Floyd cried out for his mother several times, but within eight minutes he was dead.

On March 25, 2020, Floyd had been arrested for allegedly passing a counterfeit twenty-dollar bill at a local grocery store. A store employee called police, reporting that Floyd seemed drunk and not in control of himself. Three police officers arrived on the scene, and Floyd told them he was not drunk or on drugs. He resisted getting into the police cruiser, stating that he suffered from claustrophobia and feared that the police might harm him. Floyd struggled with officers as they handcuffed him. Chauvin soon arrived and took command of the situation. It is unclear whether Chauvin yanked Floyd out of the police car or Floyd exited on his own. Whichever the case, Floyd fell to the pavement onto his chest, and Chauvin knelt on his neck, killing him.

Minneapolis Explodes

Floyd's death at age forty-six set off a major cataclysm. In the Twin Cities of Minneapolis and St. Paul, viral video of Floyd's death triggered protests almost immediately. On March 26, the day after Floyd's death, thousands of people gathered at the site. They held homemade signs that read "Black Lives Matter," "Justice for George Floyd," and "I Can't Breathe." Minneapolis police chief Medaria Arradondo fired the four officers who participated in Floyd's arrest. (Chauvin was indicted for murder several days later, facing charges that carried a forty-year maximum sentence.)

The actions taken against the officers did little to calm the situation. A large crowd again assembled at the site the next day. The protest was largely peaceful until night fell. Then demonstrators marched several miles to the Third Precinct police station, where the four officers involved in Floyd's arrest had been assigned. Some began vandalizing police cars; others surrounded the station, chanting slogans and demanding justice for Floyd. Nearby businesses, including a Target, a liquor store, and an auto-parts store, were looted. Several businesses were set on fire. Police reacted by firing tear gas and rubber bullets into the crowd. Cell phone videos taken at the time show that the looting was initiated by a masked White man carrying an umbrella. The man was later linked by Minneapolis police to a White supremacist group. According to department spokesperson Erika Christensen, "Until the actions of the . . . 'Umbrella Man,' the protests had been relatively peaceful. The actions of this person created an atmosphere of hostility and tension. . . . This individual's sole aim was to incite violence."[18]

Despite how it began, the hostility and tension continued to spin out of control. On the night of May 28, hundreds of people surrounded the Third Precinct station, hurling rocks and bottles as police defended the building with rubber ball grenades and rubber bullets. Eventually, the police abandoned the Third Precinct station, and it was set on fire as the crowd cheered. During the next two nights, seventy-five fires were reported around the city. Damage has been estimated at half a billion dollars.

Black Lives Matter activists do not support arson, vandalism, or looting; the group is dedicated to nonviolent protests. However, BLM is a decentralized group with few formal leaders. No one from Black Lives Matter was in charge of coordinating the chaotic activities during the initial George Floyd demonstrations. A few cell phone videos were taken during the Third Precinct protests and posted to social media. Activists can be heard urging people to stop vandalizing police cars and to go home. However, these people were unable to calm the angry crowd.

Social Media Spreads the Word

The George Floyd protests rapidly spread across the country, and in some areas, demonstrators focused on local killings of Black people. In Louisville, Kentucky, protestors drew attention to the death of twenty-six-year-old Breonna Taylor, who was shot seven times on March 13 during a botched police raid that wrongly targeted her home. In Atlanta, Georgia, protesters focused on the February 23 murder of Ahmaud Arbery, a twenty-five-year-old Black jogger who was shot by two White vigilantes. As with the Floyd incident, the killing was captured on cell phone video, prompting actor Will Smith to comment, "Racism is not getting worse, it's getting filmed."[19]

> "Racism is not getting worse, it's getting filmed."[19]
>
> —Will Smith, actor

In many cases it is young activists who are ensuring that the world sees those videos. They are proficient with social media, and they are using it to help organize protests and to keep the world's attention focused on police who abuse their powers. Some of the young activists leading the Black Lives Matter marches are referred to as the Trayvon Generation; they came of age between the deaths of Trayvon Martin and George Floyd. Michael-Michelle Pratt is part of the Trayvon Generation; she was twelve when Martin was killed, and his death led her to a life of activism. Pratt says:

For most of my adolescence, I've had to watch people that look like me be dehumanized and physically assaulted. . . . We were children when George Zimmerman's act of violence against Trayvon Martin went unpunished. We have marched, reblogged, retweeted, organized, volunteered, and donated. We are adults, or almost adults now. This is a boiling point and it's spilling over. Get ready![20]

Some members of the Trayvon Generation are working alongside Black Lives Matter to start their own movements. In Nashville, Tennessee, six high school students, including Jade Fuller and Nya Collins, started Teens4Equality in the wake of Floyd's

Protesting During a Pandemic

When George Floyd was killed by Minneapolis police officer Derek Chauvin on May 25, 2020, Americans were living under a lockdown put in place to stop the spread of coronavirus and the disease it causes. Schools and businesses across the country had been shut down since mid-March, leaving millions of Americans stuck at home. When the gruesome video of Chauvin kneeling on Floyd's neck appeared, it spread around the world at lightning speed. Suddenly, people who had been confined at home for months were prompted to seek justice for Floyd and all Black lives that have been impacted by systemic racism. As a result, countless Americans, including White people who had never protested before, joined together under the banner of Black Lives Matter.

Black Lives Matter activist and college professor Frank Leon Roberts says that widespread unemployment, the lockdown, and the racism displayed by Chauvin in the video created a "perfect storm for rebellion." According to Roberts, "History changes when you have an unexpected convergence of forces. . . . You have a situation where the entire country is on lockdown, and more people are inside watching TV . . . more people are being forced to pay attention—they're less able to look away, less distracted."

Quoted in Helier Cheung, "George Floyd Death: Why US Protests Are So Powerful This Time," BBC News, June 8, 2020. www.bbc.com.

death. They launched a June 4 protest on Twitter, and ten thousand people showed up. According to Fuller:

> What really sparked things up for us was we reached out to Black Lives Matter Nashville, and we asked them if they would support our protest. We started getting a lot of demand, a lot of people asking us if we wanted any donations. . . . We got a ton of donations in advance for water bottles and first aid and all of that, and then we have the legal team on our side with Black Lives Matter Nashville. All these amazing people just came together.[21]

The groups coordinating with Black Lives Matter highlight the decentralized nature of the movement. While BLM has official chapters in fifteen cities, the group's website provides resources that include social media graphics, petitions, and educational materials to anyone who wants to organize their own protests. But whatever banners the activists are marching under, the unifying force is anger over racial injustice. As twenty-year-old Minneapolis BLM organizer Van Covington puts it, "I think that everyone in Minneapolis, everyone in Minnesota, who is a Black person that lives here could have seen this coming. [We] could have seen the uprising, the riots, the burning of the precinct—we all saw this coming. . . . Minneapolis was fed up. Black youth are fed up."[22]

The Largest Protest Movement Ever

After Floyd's death it seemed as if millions of Americans of all races and religions were fed up with systemic racism and police violence against Black people. In the week that followed Floyd's death, Black Lives Matter channeled the widespread anger into public protests in one city after another. According to data compiled by Civis Analytics, on June 6 more than half a million people turned out to support Black lives in more than 550 cities. By mid-June more than two thousand protests had been held across all

Black Lives Matter became a global phenomenon as protesters rallied in one country after another. Pictured here is a Black Lives Matter protest in May 2020 in London's Trafalgar Square.

50 states. That same compilation of data showed that 15 million to 26 million Americans—of all races and ethnicities—had participated in the demonstrations. This put Black Lives Matter at the center of the largest protest movement in US history. The protests and other activities were not confined to major population centers like Minneapolis, Los Angeles, and Houston. Citizens inspired by the Black Lives Matter movement organized marches in hundreds of small towns, too. And according to Civis Analytics, 95 percent of the counties where protests occurred were majority White.

Many of the rallies in small towns were sparked by local Black organizers, like nineteen-year-old Jayden Johnson of Fort Dodge, Iowa. In 2020 Fort Dodge had a population of just over twenty-three thousand. Nearly 90 percent were White, and about 5 percent were Black. Johnson recalls that she was only eight years old when someone first yelled a racial slur at her. When she was old enough to drive, she remembers being pulled over by police without reason on a number of occasions. When Johnson saw the video of Floyd's killing, she posted a simple message on Snapchat: "Everybody meet at the [town] square at 8 p.m."[23]

No one could remember a protest march ever taking place in Fort Dodge, and Johnson expected around fifteen people to show up. Instead, she was greeted by the sight of around one hundred young adults—Black, White, Latinx, and mixed race. As Johnson recalls, "I saw people who looked like me and didn't look like me, and I started thinking, 'Something really is different now.'"[24] The activists marched down the middle of the town's main street carrying handmade signs and chanting "Black lives matter." The town's police chief, Roger Porter, said the rally was very positive and that the group got its message across.

Protests in Fort Dodge and hundreds of other small towns are a result of changing national demographics as the United States becomes what is called a majority-minority country. About half of the population under age thirty in the United States is made up of Black, Latinx, and other minorities, while in many small towns like Fort Dodge, the majority of the White population is over age fifty-five and shrinking.

Wherever the Black Lives Matter rallies have occurred, they seem to have an effect on police practices and other long-standing issues associated with systemic racism. Throughout the country, legislators have enacted new laws to regulate police conduct. The legislature in Iowa, which was controlled by conservative Republicans at the time of Floyd's death, voted to prevent police departments from hiring officers who had been fired for misconduct in other states. Lawmakers also banned the chokehold and the stranglehold. These techniques are used by police to restrain someone by maintaining a tight grip around the neck, cutting off blood flow to the brain. Floyd's death was caused by a variation of the chokehold called the neck restraint,

"I have never seen a political organization [Black Lives Matter] be able to do what they have done this quickly. . . . It could be hugely impactful to our future here."[25]

—Jessica Vanden Berg, political consultant

prompting the city of Minneapolis to ban neck holds. Iowa political consultant Jessica Vanden Berg was surprised by these actions, which activists have been demanding for years: "I have never seen a political organization [Black Lives Matter] be able to do what they have done this quickly in this state. There is now this sustained political organization of protesters, and it could be hugely impactful to our future here."[25]

BLM Goes Global

The goals of the Black Lives Matter movement resonated with people around the world; the global movement spread rapidly through the deft use of social media. Protesters carrying Black Lives Matter signs held rallies in hundreds of cities in Africa, Australia, Brazil, Japan, South Korea, the United Kingdom, and other places. In some cases, protesters sought to show solidarity with those who demanded justice for George Floyd, Breonna Taylor, and other Black Americans who were victims of police violence. In other places, protesters demonstrated against local injustices perpetrated against people in their own nations.

The guiding principles of Black Lives Matter—racial justice, income equality, and LGBTQ rights—helped people find a voice for their own causes. In Brussels, Belgium, ten thousand people turned out to protest against racism and demanded that leaders apologize for the racist policies carried out in Africa in past centuries. In Sydney, Australia, thousands demonstrated their solidarity with Black Lives Matter while protesting against their nation's harsh treatment of the nation's indigenous Aboriginal peoples.

In Tokyo, Japan, a Black twenty-five-year-old graphic designer from Maryland named Jaime Smith founded a Black Lives Matter chapter after Floyd's killing. Smith wanted to call attention to the anti-Black racism she experienced in Japan. "I've had strangers reach out and grab my hair," she says. "Strangers yell [racist insults] at me on the street. Also, my first week in this area, I got stopped by the police because I had a

Diluting the Message

As the George Floyd protests, which began in late May, continued into August, the center of the demonstrations seemed to shift to Portland, Oregon, where hundreds of young, mostly White protesters clashed with local police and federal authorities night after night. In an unprecedented move, President Donald Trump sent squads of masked, anonymous federal officers in combat fatigues to Portland to attack, detain, and arrest protesters. E.D. Mondainé, president of the Portland branch of the National Association for the Advancement of Colored People, felt the actions in Portland were diluting the message of Black Lives Matter. He says:

> Unfortunately, "spectacle" is now the best way to describe Portland's protests. Vandalizing government buildings and hurling projectiles at law enforcement draw attention—but how do these actions stop police from killing black people? What are antifa and other leftist agitators achieving for the cause of black equality? The [protest,] while perhaps well-intentioned, ends up redirecting attention away from the urgent issue of murdered black bodies. This might ease the consciences of white, affluent [people] who have previously been silent in the face of black oppression, but it's fair to ask: Are they really furthering the cause of justice?

E.D. Mondainé, "Portland's Protests Were Supposed to Be About Black Lives. Now, They're White Spectacle," *Washington Post*, July 23, 2020. www.washingtonpost.com.

new bike."[26] Smith utilized Twitter and Instagram to organize a protest, expecting around three hundred people to show up. In what turned out to be the largest protest ever held in Tokyo, over three thousand Japanese and non-Japanese people attended the demonstration. They held signs written in English and Japanese that said "Black Lives Matter" and "Discrimination Is Born from Ignorance."

In Bristol, England, protesters tore down a statue of the seventeenth-century slave trader Edward Colston. A twenty-nine-year-old British Black Lives Matter organizer named Alex explained why the movement spread so quickly around the globe:

> We stand alone in terms of creating our momentum—not just responding to what's happening in the US. . . . I think that's because we understand that what happens over there also happens over here. . . . And so we understand the connections there as well as the connections with other people and other parts of Europe. So we've also connected with groups in Germany, in France, and in Belgium recently. There's so much in common.[27]

Focus Shifts

While most BLM protests in other nations were limited in scope, the Black Lives Matter movement in the United States continued to sustain its momentum throughout the summer of 2020. By the end of August, three months after Floyd's death, seventy BLM protests per week were still occurring around the country, according to one database that uses media reports to compile data on protests. However, some of the demonstrations became chaotic and violent, shifting the focus away from the racial justice issues that had propelled Black Lives Matter into the national—and global—spotlight. This is what happened in Portland, Oregon, a city with a mostly White population and a history of political activism.

Black Lives Matter protests began almost immediately in Portland after Floyd's death. By early June some of the protests were attracting more than ten thousand people. While the rallies were largely peaceful during the day, incidents of looting, arson, and vandalism occurred at night. By July Portland's federal courthouse was the target of protesters who spray painted graffiti on

On Twitter and in speeches President Donald Trump often attacked Black Lives Matter, falsely claiming that the group supports violence, looting, and anarchy.

the building and threw fireworks at police, who responded with tear gas and rubber bullets.

The nightly clashes between protesters and police continued for more than one hundred days, igniting a political backlash. President Donald Trump saw the chaos in Portland as an opportunity to emphasize the law-and-order platform that was at the center of his reelection campaign. Throughout the summer Trump regularly attacked Black Lives Matter on Twitter. In dozens of tweets, the president falsely claimed that BLM supported violence, looting, and anarchy. In one tweet, Trump called Black Lives Matter a "symbol of hate"[28] when the city of New York moved to paint a BLM mural on the street in front of Trump Tower (the president's former residence on Fifth Avenue).

Violence, vandalism, and looting did occur at protests in Portland and in some other cities, but the extent of those actions was magnified by extensive media coverage. According to the Armed Conflict Location & Event Data Project (ACLED), which usually studies war zones and political upheaval in developing nations, BLM protests were largely peaceful. The organization analyzed 7,750 BLM protests in more than 2,400 locations in all 50 states during May 26 to August 22, 2020. The ACLED concluded that 93 percent of the events were peaceful and nondestructive. And even when protests became violent, the report states, the destruction was confined to a few blocks rather than being widespread. The ACLED also stated that when authorities beat protesters and fired tear gas and rubber bullets, it made things worse: "The heavy-handed police response appears to have inflamed tensions and increased the risk of violent escalation."[29]

Rapid Social Change

Black Lives Matter activists have continued their efforts to shine a bright light on racial injustice and to call for meaningful change. Their message has inspired Americans and people from nations around the globe. Stanford University sociology professor Douglas McAdam highlighted the influence of Black Lives Matter when he wrote, "It looks, for all the world, like these [BLM] protests are achieving what very few do: setting in motion a period of significant, sustained, and widespread social, political change. We appear to be experiencing a social change tipping point—that is as rare in society as it is potentially consequential."[30]

> "We appear to be experiencing a social change tipping point—that is as rare in society as it is potentially consequential."[30]
>
> —Douglas McAdam, professor

CHAPTER THREE

Making Demands

Black Lives Matter motivated millions of protesters to speak out against institutional bias and the excessive use of force by police in interactions with African Americans. The group's message was strongly focused on enacting police reforms. But many activists view criminal justice as only one thread in the web that makes up systemic racism. Statistics show that Black Americans face discrimination in health care, banking, employment, and education. And Black Lives Matter, which speaks with many voices to address a broad range of problems, is working to link these other issues to problems with policing.

The George Floyd protests took place during the deadly COVID-19 pandemic, a crisis that has exposed deep disparities between the races on many levels. COVID-19, the disease caused by the coronavirus, altered the lives of practically everyone as schools, stores, restaurants, and other businesses closed to stop the spread of the virus. Countless people lost their jobs and livelihoods. But people of color suffered more than Whites from effects of the pandemic. A June 2020 poll conducted by Fortune-SurveyMonkey found that Black and Hispanic workers were more than twice as likely as White workers to have lost their jobs due to the pandemic.

Even before the virus struck, the majority of Black people in the United States occupied the lower rungs of the economic ladder. Regardless of educational background, Black Americans earn less money than Whites. According to statistics compiled by the Federal Reserve Bank of Minneapolis, the median income for Black households in the United States was $38,200 in 2020, less than half that of White households ($85,400).

When the pandemic hit, it highlighted other racial disparities. Black Americans were more likely to lose their jobs than White Americans. Many who kept their jobs worked in positions with a higher risk of exposure to the virus. These workers had jobs in grocery stores, warehouses, hospitals, restaurants, and other businesses that did not allow for work from home. This has contributed to a higher COVID-related death rate for African Americans—three times higher than the death rate for White Americans, according to the APM Research Lab. In some parts of the country, the statistics are even more troubling. Blacks in Kansas are seven times more likely to die from COVID-19, while the rate is six times higher for those who live in Missouri, Wisconsin, and Washington, DC. Other factors that have added to the death toll include poverty, lack of access to medical care, and underlying health conditions (such as hypertension and diabetes) that are prevalent among Black Americans. Philosophy professor and Black activist Cornel West blames the higher rate of sickness and death on systemic racism: "The virus encounters deeply racist structures and institutions already in place, against the backdrop of wealth inequality."[31]

Defund Police?

Leaders in the Black Lives Matter movement have addressed many of these issues with the #WhatMatters2020 campaign. According to the BLM website, the campaign is meant to "build collective power and ensure [political] candidates are held accountable for the issues that systematically and disproportionately impact Black and under-served communities across the nation."[32] The BLM website addresses issues such as economic injustice, access to quality health care and education, and LGBTQ rights. The campaign calls for emergency funding for child care for working poor families, expansion of unemployment insurance and other benefits, and a moratorium on evictions and utility shutoffs during the pandemic.

Addressing all these issues would cost billions of dollars, and BLM believes that the money should come from the large budgets that maintain police departments. While the issue is complex, one proposed solution is described with a simple slogan seen on countless signs and boarded-up windows during Black Lives Matter protests: Defund the Police.

The phrase "defund the police" quickly became a contentious political issue during a heated election season. Some politicians seized on the slogan to paint protesters and their supporters as revolutionaries and criminals eager to see cities descend into lawless anarchy. Those who backed the defund movement, such as Black Lives Matter activist Mariame Kaba, argued that police funding could be used for better purposes. "We are not abandoning our communities to violence," says Kaba. "We don't want to just close police departments. We want to make them obsolete.

A long line forms outside a New York City food pantry during the COVID-19 pandemic. Millions of Americans lost jobs during the pandemic, with people of color being among the hardest hit.

We should redirect the billions that now go to police departments toward providing health care, housing, education and good jobs. If we did this, there would be less need for the police in the first place."[33]

Police departments absorb billions of dollars from city budgets. In 2020 the Center for Popular Democracy analyzed the public safety budgets of one hundred major cities. The group concluded that policing costs Americans around $115 billion annually. In many cities the single largest budget expenditure is policing. Among cities highlighted in the report was Minneapolis, where $1.6 billion, or 41 percent of city spending in 2019, went to the police department. In Los Angeles, the police department received $1.7 billion in 2020, more than a quarter of the city's total budget. Other government services receive much less money. Los Angeles, for instance, spent $81 million on housing assistance and $30 million on economic development. And police department budgets have continued to rise even as crime rates fall. According to the Federal Bureau of Investigation, violent crime fell 51 percent from 1993 to 2018, while property crimes declined by 54 percent. But as the figures from the Center for Popular Democracy show, even as cities become safer, police expenditures have remained at the same level. Put another way, police departments are spending roughly the same amount of money in 2020 as they did in the 1990s, when crime rates were much higher, according to the US Department of Justice.

> "We don't want to just close police departments. We want to make them obsolete. We should redirect the billions . . . toward providing health care, housing, education and good jobs."[33]
>
> —Mariame Kaba, Black Lives Matter activist

Racial Disparities

Black Lives Matter activists point out that police officers have long been used to enforce systemic racism. In the twentieth century, police in southern states enforced laws that prevented Black people from voting while beating and arresting those who challenged racial segregation in schools, businesses, and elsewhere.

Since the 1980s local police departments have been the main enforcers behind the war on drugs. According to the American Civil Liberties Union (ACLU), this war has been disproportionately waged against Black people. Blacks are three times more likely to be arrested for drug possession even though they use drugs at the same rate as Whites. And while Black people constitute 13 percent of the population, they make up 29 percent of those arrested for drug crimes and 40 percent of those incarcerated for drug law violations. Like all convicted felons, Black people who have served time in prison continue to be punished when released. They are denied employment opportunities, business loans, student aid, public housing, and other social and economic benefits.

Activists believe that the money used to arrest, convict, and jail drug users would be better spent on public health and education. As ACLU policing policy adviser Paige Fernandez explains, "By shrinking [the] massive budgets [of police departments], we can help end decades of racially driven social control and oppression as well as address social problems at their root instead of investing in an institution that further oppresses and terrorizes communities."[34]

After the protests following George Floyd's death, some cities moved to redirect money from police departments to other city services. The city council in Austin, Texas, cut $150 million from the police budget, about one-third of the money it typically receives. The money was directed to social programs that focus on violence prevention and food security. Officials in Los Angeles also cut around $150 million, which amounts to about 9 percent of the city's overall police department budget. In New York City, council members voted to cut $1 billion from the city's $6 billion annual police budget. Officials in Seattle, Baltimore, Philadelphia, Washington, DC, and elsewhere also redirected spending away from police departments.

"By shrinking [the] massive budgets [of police departments], we can help end decades of racially driven social control and oppression as well as address social problems at their root."[34]

—Paige Fernandez, American Civil Liberties Union policing policy adviser

Calling for Community Oversight

Campaign Zero, a project launched by Black Lives Matter, strives to eliminate police killings. One way for this to happen, the group believes, is for police departments to take citizen complaints of police misconduct more seriously. Toward that end, the group urges all police departments to establish a Civilian Complaints Office that would do the following:

- receive, investigate and resolve all civilian complaints against police in 120 days
- establish multiple in-person and online ways to submit, view and discuss complaints
- be immediately notified and required to send an investigator to the scene of a police shooting or in-custody death
- be allowed to interrogate officers less than 48 hours after an incident where deadly force is used
- access crime scenes, subpoena witnesses and files with penalties for non-compliance
- make disciplinary and policy recommendations to the Police Chief
- compel the Police Chief to explain why he/she has not followed a recommendation . . .
- be funded at an amount no less than 5% of the total police department budget
- have at least 1 investigator for every 70 police officers or 4 investigators

Campaign Zero, "Community Oversight," 2020. www.joincampaignzero.org.

Taking On Police Unions

As might be expected, many police officers—from cops on the street to police chiefs—rejected the idea of defunding their departments. And in most major cities, the demands made by police officers are backed by powerful unions that represent the interests of law enforcement. Police unions negotiate strict contracts with city officials that make it nearly impossible for police departments to fire or even punish officers who misbehave or break the law.

Most police union contracts feature disciplinary protections for union members; that is, the contracts protect officers who have been charged with improper use of force and other wrongdoing. These stipulations are based on the idea that criminal suspects will make false accusations of misconduct against officers in order to get their case dismissed. However, when officers are found to have acted improperly, their union contracts often protect them. Disciplinary actions might be kept secret from the press and the public or erased from the record after several years. When an officer shoots

Reform and Respect

Many Black Lives Matter activists at the George Floyd protests carried signs that said "defund the police." But according to a June 2020 poll by Yahoo News/YouGov, there is strong support for police funding in communities where crime and violence remain a daily fact of life. The poll found that 50 percent of Black respondents agreed with the statement "We need more cops on the street." At the same time, 49 percent of Black people polled said they feel less secure when they see a police officer. This contradiction reveals the complex feelings of many whose concerns cannot be reduced to a simple slogan like "defund the police." Sondra and Don Samuels are married Black activists in Minneapolis who sued the city after the George Floyd killing because they felt the police did not adequately protect their neighborhood during the uprising that followed. The Samuelses explain that, while they do not support defunding police, "we want radical police reform, where all citizens are treated as fully human by all cops. . . . We support the reform . . . which include[s] community alternatives to policing that work hand-in-hand with our police force. African Americans, especially, desire a relationship with our cops of mutual respect, support and accountability."

Sondra Samuels and Don Samuels, "Why We Northside Neighbors Are Suing Minneapolis," *Minneapolis (MN) Star Tribune*, August 24, 2020. www.startribune.com.

someone or uses force, many contracts include a forty-eight-hour waiting period before the officer can be interviewed about the incident. Critics say this gives police who engage in violent conduct time to develop a strategy to avoid responsibility. They can consult with officers who were witnesses to create a unified description of the action that in some cases might not be true.

Derek Chauvin, who killed George Floyd, benefited from police union protections. During his nineteen years on the force, Chauvin was subjected to at least seventeen misconduct complaints, including pulling a gun on a group of teenagers who were playing with a toy gun. Chauvin was also involved in three shootings, one of them fatal. But Chauvin's union contract prevented Minneapolis from taking any serious disciplinary actions against him. Justice Department lawyer Jonathan M. Smith explains how this led to tragedy: "Had those [incidents] been addressed in an appropriate way, not only would Mr. Floyd be alive, we wouldn't have the disruption in the community and you might have actually saved [Chauvin's] career if you put him on the right path earlier on."[35]

Most police union leaders, who also work as officers, are White; of the fifteen largest American cities, only Memphis, Tennessee, has a Black union leader. And after the Floyd protests began, many union leaders came out in strong opposition to police reforms. This includes Bob Kroll, who leads the Police Officers Federation of Minneapolis. Kroll has been accused of making racist remarks on a number of occasions. During the 2020 Minneapolis George Floyd protests, he referred to Black Lives Matter as a "terrorist organization."[36]

In 2015 Black Lives Matter launched a program called Campaign Zero to reduce the number of police shootings to zero. One of the Campaign Zero initiatives challenges the power of police unions. According to the organization, 84 percent of police union contracts impose one or more barriers to police accountability. A Campaign Zero report on police unions states, "Police union contracts . . . have created a system of protections for police officers that amount to an alternate justice system, creating significant legal and structural barriers to accountability, transparency, and fairness."[37]

In 2020 Campaign Zero created a program called #NIXTHE6 to challenge six ways it says police unions obstruct, delay, or defeat local efforts to hold police accountable. The campaign is promoting what it calls fair police contracts. These contracts would require preservation of police misconduct records and make them available to the public.

Qualified Immunity

Campaign Zero believes that the best way to reform policing is to pressure elected officials at every level of the government to enact policies that address police misconduct. The group tracks state, local, and federal legislation and calls on supporters to demand action from lawmakers. One major federal bill supported by Campaign Zero was called the George Floyd Justice in Policing Act. The act was passed by the House of Representatives in 2020 but stalled in the Senate. It would have restricted the use of military equipment by police departments, required all officers to wear body cameras, and impelled police departments to adopt antidiscrimination training programs. The George Floyd Justice in Policing Act also addressed a legal concept called qualified immunity. This little-known court ruling protects officers from lawsuits and financial penalties, even when police use excessive force or kill innocent people.

The concept of qualified immunity is the result of a 1967 Supreme Court ruling. In that ruling, the court determined that police officers could not be sued for violating the rights of civil rights protesters in the South. The ruling was meant to protect officials who were acting in good faith, such as police officers making life-and-death decisions while performing their jobs. The court stated that officials were shielded from liability in lawsuits unless they violated clearly established federal laws. (Qualified immunity does not protect cities, counties, and states from lawsuits based on police misconduct. In 2019 government bodies paid out over $300 million nationally to settle claims by civilians who contended they were mistreated by police.)

Since the creation of qualified immunity, thousands of lawsuits against police misconduct have been dismissed by judges.

Countless other cases were never pursued by lawyers, who were aware that officials were protected by the ruling. David Cole, legal director of the ACLU, called qualified immunity "a free pass [for police officers] to violate constitutional rights without being held to account."[38]

Qualified immunity was a relatively obscure legal doctrine until BLM opposition to it emerged during the George Floyd protests. Some of the opposition came from a coalition of 450 musicians, singers, and managers who wanted to support Black Lives Matter. The coalition, which included musical superstars like Lizzo, Rihanna, Billie Eilish, and Justin Bieber, signed an open letter to Congress in support of the George Floyd Justice in Policing Act. Singer Aloe Blacc created a smaller group within the coalition to focus solely on ending qualified immunity by applying political pressure to senators. "We really encourage [senators] to

> "[Qualified immunity is] a free pass [for police officers] to violate constitutional rights without being held to account."[38]
>
> —David Cole, American Civil Liberties Union legal director

The Black Lives Matter movement has given many Americans a new understanding of systemic racism, says cofounder Patrisse Cullors (pictured in 2018).

recognize that the change that [they] can make is to end qualified immunity," says Blacc. "We were able to put together a list of empirical data to illustrate what is wrong with qualified immunity, and why only two out of 30 cases that have gone to the higher levels of courts have ever resulted in any remedy for victims. That's a very, very poor batting average."[39]

In June 2020, even as Black Lives Matter supporters lobbied Congress, the issue of qualified immunity was before the Supreme Court at the height of the Floyd protests. The court was asked to rule on seven cases of police misconduct that had occurred years before Floyd's death. However, the court chose not to take up the cases, leaving qualified immunity in place as a guiding legal principle. Supreme Court justice Sonia Sotomayor, who dissented in the case, has long disagreed with the idea of qualified immunity, describing it as "sanctioning a shoot-first, think-later approach to policing."[40]

Advancing the BLM Agenda

Black Lives Matter has sought to do more than draw attention to individual killings. It has prompted a national discussion about other long-ignored issues affecting Black Americans, including disparities in health care, housing, education, economics, and incarceration. Patrisse Cullors explains how BLM changed the way Americans think about systemic racism:

> When I co-founded Black Lives Matter almost seven years ago, the conversation about police brutality was just beginning to enter the mainstream discourse—not because police violence was anything new, but because of the work of activists and advocates who brought the issue to light. . . . Today, more people are rallying for Black Lives than I would have ever imagined. That in itself is a sign of progress. But . . . let's make sure that Black life matters at every stage and in every facet of society, well before a cop has his knee on a man's neck.[41]

CHAPTER FOUR

Speaking Truth, Changing Minds

The large-scale Black Lives Matter demonstrations against police violence held in 2020 were unique for their rainbow of diversity. Protesters of every race, religion, ethnicity, and sexual orientation could be found marching in support of Black lives. But perhaps the most notable aspect of the movement was the age of the demonstrators. According to a study by the Pew Research Center, more than 40 percent of BLM protesters were age eighteen to twenty-nine, even though this demographic makes up only 19 percent of the US population. And thousands of students younger than eighteen also participated in the marches. While some were motivated to march by news stories and videos on social media, others had taken part in programs offered by Black Lives Matter at School. This group, loosely associated with Black Lives Matter, is focused on educating students about racial injustice, income disparity, gender inequality, and other issues.

Black Lives Matter at School first gained national attention in October 2016 when three thousand educators in the Seattle school system entered their classrooms wearing T-shirts that said, "Black Lives Matter: We Stand Together." The teachers were joined by thousands of parents and students who were protesting the police killing of Philando Castile and other Black Americans.

"I learned so much, so much, that really empowered me as a black male. This was probably the first time I was really excited about school."[42]

—Israel Presley, student activist

The actions taken in Seattle inspired thousands of teachers and students in other cities to express their support for Black Lives Matter at School. By 2017 the BLM at School movement had spread to more than twenty cities, including Philadelphia, Los Angles, Detroit, Boston, and New York City. During February 2017, in what was called the Week of Action, thousands of teachers across the country—wearing BLM T-shirts—taught lessons about structural racism, Black history, and related topics. The Week of Action became an annual event. In a 2019 video, Seattle student activist Israel Presley described how the experience motivated him: "I learned so much, so much, that really empowered me as a black male. This was probably the first time I was really excited about school."[42]

After the uprisings that followed the murders of George Floyd, Breonna Taylor, Ahmaud Arbery, and so many others in 2020, BLM at School proposed activities that expanded the Week of Action into what it called the Year of Purpose. While many schools remained closed due to the coronavirus pandemic, BLM at School provided focused lessons that could be taught to students who were attending school online. Programs for the 2020–2021 school year included Justice for George Day. On George Floyd's birthday, October 14, Floyd was remembered as teachers discussed issues like defunding the police and redirecting money to education and social programs. During National Library Week (the second week in April), BLM at School provides lesson plans for the Revolutionary Black Arts program. This curriculum highlights contributions of Black authors such as Zora Neale Hurston, Augusta Savage, and Faith Ringgold. Various other activities held throughout the school year include Student Activist Day, Education for Liberation Day, Queer Organizing Behind the Scenes, and Black Radical Educator Day.

Undoing Everyday Racism

Discussions about racial injustice, prompted by the Black Lives Matter movement, are taking place in thousands of schools. Activists hope these conversations will change the way people view the struggles Black communities have been dealing with for years. And public support for Black Lives Matter has spurred conversations about racism beyond the classroom and to living rooms across the country. According to a June 2020 Monmouth University poll, 49 percent of Americans agreed with the statement that police are more likely to use excessive force against Black suspects. In 2016 only 25 percent believed that to be true.

As more White people struggled to learn about systemic racism, Ibram X. Kendi's 2019 book, *How to Be an Antiracist*, became a best seller. According to Kendi, antiracism focuses on identifying the numerous acts of intentional and unintentional racism Black people encounter on a daily basis. While the term

Young protest leaders have been at the forefront of many Black Lives Matter marches. One poll found that more than 40 percent of protesters have been between the ages of eighteen and twenty-nine.

"The only way to undo racism is to consistently identify and describe it—and then dismantle it."[43]

—Ibram X. Kendi. director of Boston University's Center for Antiracist Research

antiracism has been in use among academics for decades, the concept was never widely discussed until the Black Lives Matter protests in 2020. Kendi, the founding director of Boston University's Center for Antiracist Research, explains the goals of antiracism: "The only way to undo racism is to consistently identify and describe it—and then dismantle it."[43]

The difficulty with dismantling racism is that racist concepts have long been seen as a normal aspect of American culture. For example, as president, Donald Trump used the language of racism when criticizing people he disagreed with. This helped normalize racist ideas that were once considered abhorrent. In 2020, during the George Floyd demonstrations, Trump called Black Lives Matter protesters "Looters, thugs . . . and other forms of Lowlife & Scum." Reporters pointed out that those terms have long been used by racists against Black people who were demanding equal rights. Trump answered, as he often had in the past, that he was "the least racist person there is anywhere in the world."[44]

While Trump's words might have been extraordinary for a modern American president, such denials are common. No one wants to be accused of being racist. Even prominent leaders of White supremacist groups like the Proud Boys and the Ku Klux Klan claim they are not racists. But according to Kendi:

The opposite of "racist" isn't "not racist." It is "antiracist." What's the difference? . . . One either believes problems are rooted in groups of people, as a racist, or locates the roots of problems in power and policies, as an antiracist. One either allows racial inequities to persevere, as a racist, or confronts racial inequities, as an antiracist. There is no in-between safe space of "not racist." The claim of "not racist" neutrality is a mask for racism. . . . The attempt to

46

turn this usefully descriptive term [racist] into an almost unusable slur is, of course, designed to do the opposite: to freeze us into inaction.[45]

Those who teach antiracism often focus on what is called White privilege. This term addresses the fact that society defines White customs, culture, and beliefs as normal, while nonwhite people are considered outsiders, or abnormal. As author Toni Morrison says about the United States: "In this country, American means white."[46] Concepts of whiteness and antiracism are explored in the Talking About Race series on the website of the National Museum of African American History and Culture in Washington, DC: "Persons who identify as white rarely have to think about their racial identity because they live within a culture where whiteness has been normalized. Thinking about race is very different for nonwhite persons

Misplaced Empathy

During the Black Lives Matter protests of 2020 White protesters often outnumbered Black protesters in places like Portland, Oregon, and Denver, Colorado. Some of these demonstrations featured mass "die-ins." At these events hundreds of people lay on the grass while chanting "I can't breathe" for nine minutes. These die-ins were meant to draw attention to the police killing of George Floyd in Minneapolis. But some Black activists would prefer that White supporters not show empathy by pretending to know what it feels like to be Black. BLM cofounder Alicia Garza has this view. She has said, "Don't say you can't breathe, because you can breathe just fine. You live in communities with clean air, with water you can drink likely from the tap. You can jog with earphones and a hoodie on, and no car is going to drive up on you and perform a citizen's arrest or shoot you. Nobody is going to bust in your house performing a raid and shoot you while you're asleep." Instead she has urged White supporters to use their energy to push for political and social changes.

Quoted in Stacey Patton, "White People Are Speaking Up at Protests. How Do We Know They Mean What They Say?," *Washington Post*, June 9, 2020. www.washingtonpost.com.

living in America. People of color must always consider their racial identity, whatever the situation, due to the systemic and interpersonal racism that still exists."[47]

Corporations Respond

In a society where whiteness is normalized, people of color must deal with racist stereotypes that have long been a fixed feature of American culture. Stereotypes—widely held, simplified ideas about a particular race or gender—are found in books, movies, advertising, digital media, and even on grocer's shelves. After the George Floyd protests began, media corporations, food companies, and technology platforms scrambled to remove names and brand logos that amplify racist stereotypes. Most of these gestures are symbolic and might not have a major effect on Black lives. However, the moves demonstrate the growing power of Black Lives Matter.

About a month into the George Floyd protests, Quaker Oats announced it was retiring the Aunt Jemima brand of pancake

The original Aunt Jemima image, a stereotypical Black mammy, has been updated over the years, but the brand name was unchanged. In 2020, responding to the national dialogue on race, Quaker Oats agreed to change the brand's name and logo.

mixes and syrups, which have been on grocer's shelves since 1893. Activists have long complained about the brand's name and logo, based on the stereotype of a mammy, a Black female servant who cooks for White children. As sociology professor David Pilgrim explains, "The mammy image served the political, social, and economic interests of mainstream white America. During slavery, the mammy caricature was posited as proof that blacks—in this case, black women—were contented, even happy, as slaves. Her wide grin, hearty laugher, and loyal servitude were offered as evidence of the supposed humanity of the institution of slavery."[48] While Quaker Oats updated the Aunt Jemima caricature several times in recent decades, critics felt the brand continued to normalize bigoted stereotypes.

Hours after the Aunt Jemima announcement, another longtime brand was retired. Packaging for Uncle Ben's rice, a brand owned by Mars Inc., featured another stereotype: a happy Black chef. Those who criticized the brand point out that the terms *uncle* and *aunt* were often used in the past so that White southerners could avoid calling Black people by the respectful titles *mister* or *missus*. When announcing the change in its popular brand, Mars released a statement: "Racism has no place in society. We stand in solidarity with the Black community, our Associates and our partners in the fight for social justice. We know to make the systemic change needed, it's going to take a collective effort from all of us—individuals, communities and organizations of all sizes around the world."[49]

After Uncle Ben's and Aunt Jemima were dropped, other companies followed the precedent. Conagra said it would revamp its Mrs. Butterworth's packaging, which was based on the mammy stereotype. And the company that makes Cream of Wheat cereal said it would discontinue the use of the Black character on the package, which was seen as a racist caricature. While these acts might seem trivial, these companies have spent hundreds of millions of dollars over the decades developing their logos and packaging, which are instantly recognizable wherever the products are sold.

One the most stunning examples of BLM's growing influence was seen in July 2020 when the Washington Redskins football team announced it was changing its name. The name is a racial slur used to refer to Native Americans. Activists had been calling on team owner Daniel Snyder to change the name for more than twenty years. Snyder strongly resisted activist efforts, but the final decision came down to money. FedEx, which holds the franchise's stadium naming rights, said it would refuse to pay $45 million it had promised on the deal if the team kept the name. Other major National Football League sponsors, including PepsiCo and Bank of America, threatened to pull team sponsorship.

Removing Confederate Monuments

Racist concepts promoted by football mascots and breakfast products have been around for so long as to be nearly invisible to many Americans. This is also true of the more than fifteen hundred public monuments and memorials in the United States that honor Confederate leaders and soldiers, like Jefferson Davis and Robert E. Lee. Although these men fought to preserve slavery in the South during the Civil War, statues honoring them and other Confederates can be found in town squares, in front of courthouses, and even in the US Capitol Building. And ten American military bases bear the names of Confederate generals who engaged in treason against the United States and lost.

Many Americans believe Confederate monuments were erected shortly after the Civil War ended in 1865, but this is not the case. An overwhelming majority were built in the early twentieth century. During this period the civil rights of Black people were under severe attack. White politicians in the South enacted hundreds of laws to segregate Black people and deny them voting rights. At the same time, a group called the United Daughters of the Confederacy led a movement to build more than four hundred monuments to Confederates. Another round of Confederate statue building took place during 1920 to 1940, when Black Americans were fighting against a wave of lynching across the South.

As history professor Jane Dailey explains, "Those were very clearly white supremacist monuments and are designed to intimidate, not just memorialize."[50]

Black activists have tried and failed for years to have Confederate monuments removed from public property. During the 2020 Black Lives Matter demonstrations, protesters focused their anger on Confederate monuments that were viewed as symbols of historic oppression. In Alabama, Arkansas, Florida, Georgia, Kentucky, Texas, Virginia, and elsewhere, dozens of Confederate statues were knocked off their pedestals by protesters. Some activists did not support these actions; they felt that those who destroyed public property were distracting from the main BLM message aimed at halting police killings. However, the call to remove the Confederate symbols resonated in the halls of city governments throughout the country, where politicians

> "[Confederate monuments are] very clearly white supremacist monuments and are designed to intimidate, not just memorialize."[50]
>
> —Jane Dailey, history professor

Following an order by North Carolina's governor, a worker removes a Confederate monument from the state capitol grounds in Raleigh in June 2020. Similar actions took place in other southern cities.

voted to remove the statues and monuments in public places. By June 2020 the symbols of the Confederacy were taken down in at least twenty-two cities, including Mobile, Alabama; Louisville, Kentucky; Richmond, Virginia; and Jacksonville, Florida.

Even in the US Senate, politicians were swept up in the anti-monument momentum. The annual bill to fund the military contained a provision to rename the bases that carried the names of Confederate generals. And Speaker of the House Nancy Pelosi ordered the removal of statues of Confederate leaders in the US

Canceling *Cops*

The reality TV show *Cops* was canceled in 2020. The action followed years of complaints about the show, which first aired in 1989. Critics said *Cops* glorified police violence against people of color, often depicting real police officers aggressively targeting poor people for minor crimes. Some said *Cops* was racially biased, representing Black people as criminals in numbers that far outweigh their percentage of the population. Despite the objections, calls for the show's cancellation were ignored. But 2020 marked the turning point, thanks to the Black Lives Matter movement. According to the civil rights organization Color of Change:

> For more than 30 years, *Cops* has miseducated the public and normalized injustice. Crime television encourages the public to accept the norms of over-policing and excessive force and reject reform, while supporting the exact behavior that destroys the lives of Black people. *Cops* led the way, pushing troubling implications for generations of viewers. . . . In a moment when everyone wants to proclaim that Black Lives Matter, we must hold these companies accountable to put actions to words with a complete industry overhaul.

Quoted in Matt Miller, "Let's Topple the Racist Moments of Culture Too," *Esquire*, June 11, 2020. www.esquire.com.

Capitol. According to Pelosi, "There is no room in the hallowed halls of Congress or in any place of honor for memorializing men who embody the violent bigotry and grotesque racism of the Confederacy."[51]

Trump and others railed against removing statues and renaming the bases. They claim that the monuments are part of America's great national heritage. But according to a 2020 Quinnipiac poll, 52 percent of Americans support taking down the statues. Just three years earlier, only 39 percent expressed support for this action. That represents a large change in thinking in a very short time.

In 2020 Black Lives Matter educated a lot of Americans about racism in the United States. Dozens of companies, including Walmart, Target, Uber, Airbnb, Google, and Amazon, posted statements in support of Black Lives Matter and donated money to its cause. While public support for the movement goes up and down depending on the day's headlines, there is little doubt that the expressions of pain, rage, and frustration felt by Black Americans will make elevation of antiracism the defining cause of the 2020s.

SOURCE NOTES

Introduction: Good Trouble

1. Quoted in Aaron Morrison, "How the Black Lives Matter Generation Remembers John Lewis," ABC News, July 19, 2020. https://abcnews.go.com.
2. Quoted in Cydney Henderson, "'John Lewis: Good Trouble': 5 Lessons from the Documentary That Still Apply Today," *USA Today*, July 18, 2020. https://eu.usatoday.com.
3. John Lewis, "Together, You Can Redeem the Soul of Our Nation," *New York Times*, July 30, 2020. www.nytimes.com.

Chapter One: #BlackLivesMatter

4. Barack Obama, "Remarks by the President on Trayvon Martin," White House, July 19, 2013. https://obamawhitehouse.archives.gov.
5. Quoted in Jamil Smith, "How the Movement That's Changing America Was Built and Where It Goes Next," *Rolling Stone*, June 16, 2020. www.rollingstone.com.
6. Quoted in Smith, "How the Movement That's Changing America Was Built and Where It Goes Next."
7. Eddie S. Glaude Jr., *Democracy in Black: How Race Still Enslaves the American Soul*. New York: Broadway, 2017, p. 31.
8. Sharon LaFraniere and Andrew W. Lehren, "The Disproportionate Risk of Driving While Black," *New York Times*, October 24, 2015. www.nytimes.com.
9. Quoted in LaFraniere and Lehren, "The Disproportionate Risk of Driving While Black."
10. *Washington Post*, "Fatal Force," October 12, 2020. www.washingtonpost.com.
11. Julia Craven, "There Is No Justice in America for Black People Killed by Cops," Huffpost, June 16, 2017. www.huffpost.com.

12. Quoted in Eyder Peralta, "Philando Castile's Girlfriend Speaks Out: 'I Need Justice, I Need Peace,'" NPR, July 7, 2016. www.npr.org.

13. Quoted in T. Rees Shapiro et al., "Police Group: Minn. Governor 'Exploited What Was Already a Horrible and Tragic Situation,'" *Washington Post*, July 9, 2016. www.washingtonpost.com.

14. Quoted in Darren Sands, "Many Black Lives Matter Movement Leaders Worry Dallas Will Hurt Their Cause," Buzzfeed, July 8, 2016. www.buzzfeednews.com.

15. Quoted in Des Bieler, "NBA Superstars Issue 'Call to Action' for Fellow Athletes in Appearance at ESPYs," *Washington Post*, July 13, 2016. www.washingtonpost.com.

16. Quoted in Adia Robinson, "After 5 Years, Black Lives Matter Inspires New Protest Movements," ABC News, July 21, 2018. https://abcnews.go.com.

Chapter Two: A Force to Be Reckoned With

17. Quoted in Andre M. Perry and Tawanna Black, "George Floyd's Death Demonstrates the Policy Violence That Devalues Black Lives," Brookings Institution, May 28, 2020. www.brookings.edu.

18. Quoted in Libor Jany, "Minneapolis Police Say 'Umbrella Man' Was a White Supremacist Trying to Incite George Floyd Rioting," *Minneapolis (MN) Star Tribune*, July 28, 2020. www.startribune.com.

19. Quoted in Ed Pratt, "Racism Has Always Been Around. Now It's Being Filmed for All to See," *Baton Rouge (LA) Advocate*, May 29, 2020. www.theadvocate.com.

20. Michael-Michelle Pratt, "Growing Up Black Between Trayvon Martin and George Floyd Has My Generation at a Boiling Point," *Teen Vogue*, June 5, 2020. www.teenvogue.com.

21. Quoted in Precious Fondren, "Young Black Activists Are Leading the Movement for Black Lives," *Teen Vogue*, July 9, 2020. www.teenvogue.com.

22. Quoted in Fondren, "Young Black Activists Are Leading the Movement for Black Lives."

23. Quoted in Tim Craig and Aaron Williams, "A New Generation Challenges the Heartland," *Washington Post*, July 11, 2020. www.washingtonpost.com.
24. Quoted in Craig and Williams, "A New Generation Challenges the Heartland."
25. Quoted in Craig and Williams, "A New Generation Challenges the Heartland."
26. Quoted in Bianca Hillier, "BLM Tokyo Tackles Japan's Own Issues with Anti-Black Racism," PRI, September 16, 2020. www.pri.org.
27. Quoted in Jen Kirby, "'Black Lives Matter' Has Become a Global Rallying Cry Against Racism and Police Brutality," Vox, June 12, 2020. www.vox.com.
28. Quoted in Kevin Liptak and Kristen Holmes, "Trump Calls Black Lives Matter a 'Symbol of Hate' as He Digs In on Race," CNN, July 1, 2020. www.cnn.com.
29. Quoted in Tim Craig, "'The United States Is in Crisis': Report Tracks Thousands of Summer Protests, Most Nonviolent," *Washington Post*, September 3, 2020. www.washingtonpost.com.
30. Quoted in Larry Buchanan et al., "Black Lives Matter May Be the Largest Movement in U.S. History," *New York Times*, July 3, 2020. www.nytimes.com.

Chapter Three: Making Demands

31. Quoted in Ed Pilkington, "As 100,000 Die, the Virus Lays Bare America's Brutal Fault Lines—Race, Gender, Poverty and Broken Politics," *The Guardian* (Manchester, UK), May 29, 2020. www.theguardian.com.
32. Black Lives Matter, "BLM's #WhatMatters2020," 2020. https://blacklivesmatter.com.
33. Quoted in Aaron Ross Coleman, "How Black People Really Feel About the Police, Explained," Vox, June 17, 2020. www.vox.com.
34. Paige Fernandez, "Defunding the Police Will Actually Make Us Safer," American Civil Liberties Union, June 11, 2020. www.aclu.org.

35. Quoted in Melissa Segura, "There's One Big Reason Why Police Brutality Is So Common in the US. And That's the Police Unions," Buzzfeed, June 1, 2020. www.buzzfeednews.com.
36. Quoted in Samantha Michaels, "Minneapolis Police Union President Allegedly Wore a 'White Power Patch' and Made Racist Remarks," *Mother Jones*, May 30, 2020. www.motherjones.com.
37. DeRay McKesson et al., "Police Union Contracts and Police Bill of Rights Analysis," Campaign Zero, June 29, 2016. https://static1.squarespace.com.
38. Quoted in Hailey Fuchs, "Qualified Immunity Protection for Police Emerges as a Flash Point Amid Protests," *New York Times*, June 23, 2020. www.nytimes.com.
39. Quoted in Jon Blistein, "Aloe Blacc: The Police Have Hid Behind 'Qualified Immunity' for Too Long," *Rolling Stone*, July 2, 2020. www.rollingstone.com.
40. Quoted in Ben Embry, "Why Now Is the Time to End Qualified Immunity," The Pitch, July 13, 2020. www.thepitchkc.com.
41. Patrisse Cullors, "'Black Lives Matter' Is About More than the Police," American Civil Liberties Union, June 23, 2020. www.aclu.org.

Chapter Four: Speaking Truth, Changing Minds

42. Quoted in Valerie Strauss, "It's 'Black Lives Matter at School Week': Why That Matters, and How Classrooms Are Taking Part," *Washington Post*, February 5, 2019. www.washingtonpost.com.
43. Quoted in Hillary Hoffower, "What It Really Means to Be an Anti-racist, and Why It's Not the Same as Being an Ally," Business Insider, June 8, 2020. www.businessinsider.com.
44. Quoted in Andrea González-Ramírez, "The Ever-Growing List of Trump's Most Racist Rants," Medium, June 2020. https://gen.medium.com.
45. Ibram X. Kendi, *How to Be an Antiracist*. New York: One World, 2019, p. 9.
46. Quoted in "Talking about Race: Whiteness," National Museum of African American History and Culture, 2020. https://nmaahc.si.edu.
47. "Talking about Race: Whiteness," National Museum of African American History and Culture.

48. David Pilgrim, "The Mammy Caricature," Ferris State University, 2012. www.ferris.edu.
49. Quoted in Doha Madani, "Uncle Ben's Rice to Change Brand as Part of Parent Company's Stance Against Racism," NBC News, June 17, 2020. www.nbcnews.com.
50. Quoted in Ryan Best, "Confederate Statues Were Never Really About Preserving History," FiveThirtyEight, July 8, 2020. https://projects.fivethirtyeight.com.
51. Quoted in Chris Cillizza, "SIREN: A Majority of Americans Now Back Removing Confederate Statues," CNN, June 18, 2020. www.cnn.com.

ORGANIZATIONS AND WEBSITES

Black Lives Matter (BLM)

https://blacklivesmatter.com

The BLM website features news about the movement and information about the latest protests and other actions. Users can download tool kits with learning materials about conflict resolution, race relations, and COVID-19.

Black Lives Matter at School

www.blacklivesmatteratschool.com

Black Lives Matter at School is a national coalition working to promote racial justice in education. The group provides free teaching materials to promote the movement's message among students in every age group.

Color of Change

https://colorofchange.org

Color of Change is one of the nation's largest online racial justice organizations. The group's comprehensive website features news, educational materials, and strategic initiatives supporters can join to expand voting rights and workers' rights and to reform police departments.

Ibram X. Kendi

www.ibramxkendi.com

Kendi is an award-winning, best-selling author and founding director of the Boston University Center for Antiracist Research. His website features essays, articles, podcasts, videos, and other media focused on antiracism, the Black Lives Matter movement, White privilege, and other issues of interest to activists.

NAACP Legal Defense and Educational Fund
www.naacpldf.org

This arm of the National Association for the Advancement of Colored People focuses on achieving racial justice through litigation, advocacy, and public education. The website contains information about police and criminal justice reform, challenges to voting rights, and legal struggles for equal education.

National Museum of African American History and Culture
https://nmaahc.si.edu

The only national museum devoted to African American life and history features a wealth of online resources for students and teachers, including the Talking About Race web series that addresses structural racism, Whiteness, antiracism, and other prominent topics brought to the fore during the BLM protests of 2020.

Books

Tiffany Jewell, *This Book Is Anti-racist: 20 Lessons on How to Wake Up, Take Action, and Do the Work*. London: Frances Lincoln Children's Books, 2020.

Ibram X. Kendi, *How to Be an Antiracist*. New York: One World, 2019.

Peggy J. Parks, *The Black Lives Matter Movement*. San Diego: ReferencePoint, 2018.

Amy Reed, ed., *Our Stories, Our Voices: 21 YA Authors Get Real About Injustice, Empowerment, and Growing Up Female in America*. New York: Simon Pulse, 2018.

Jason Reynolds and Ibram X. Kendi, *Stamped: Racism, Antiracism, and You: A Remix of the National Book Award–Winning Stamped from the Beginning*. New York: Little, Brown Books for Young Readers, 2020.

Ibi Zoboi, ed., *Black Enough: Stories of Being Young & Black in America*. New York: Balzer + Bray, 2020.

Internet Sources

Ryan Best, "Confederate Statues Were Never Really About Preserving History," FiveThirtyEight, July 8, 2020. https://projects .fivethirtyeight.com.

Andrea González-Ramírez, "The Ever-Growing List of Trump's Most Racist Rants," Medium, June 2020. https://gen.medium .com.

Barack Obama, "Remarks by the President on Trayvon Martin," White House, July 19, 2013. https://obamawhitehouse.archives.gov.

Jamil Smith, "How the Movement That's Changing America Was Built and Where It Goes Next," *Rolling Stone*, June 16, 2020. www .rollingstone.com.

INDEX